~~Wigginton~~ High School

Adolf Hitler

MIKE WILSON

Published in association with The Basic Skills Agency

Hodder & Stoughton
A MEMBER OF THE HODDER HEADLINE GROUP

It is hard to explain
the rise and fall of Adolf Hitler.

In 1914, he was a homeless tramp.
Twenty years later,
he was head of state in Germany.

By 1941, he ruled most of Europe.
Four years later he killed himself,
with only a few followers at his side.

There was only one woman in his life.
She killed herself.

What kind of man
was the real Adolf Hitler?

Homeless

Adolf Hitler was born on April 20, 1889,
in a small town near Linz in Austria.

His father was 52 when Adolf was born,
and died when his son was still a boy.
His mother died when he was 18.

Young Adolf didn't do very well at school,
mainly because he was lazy.
He failed his school leaving exams.

He wanted to get in to Art College,
but was turned down again and again.

For five years, from 1909 to 1914,
Hitler lived in a hostel in Vienna,
with tramps and beggars,
men with no hope.

The start of the First World War, in 1914,
was Hitler's escape.
He joined the Army.

Hitler was brave in the War,
and was awarded the Iron Cross.

But the army thought
he was a "know-all and grumbler".
He was still only a corporal
when the war ended in 1918.

The First World War ended in disaster
for Germany.

Many Germans felt shame and anger
when they lost the war.
They were poor and hungry,
and there were no jobs.

Hitler knew the time was right
to start to fight back.
He decided to become a politician.

Power

Hitler found it was easy to get people,
who were fed up and angry,
to join his new party, the Nazi Party.

By 1923 there were 55,000 Nazis,
and the quick success went to Hitler's head.

In November that year,
he tried to take power in Munich.
He failed, and was put in prison.

Within a year, he was free again,
and he was stronger than ever.

In less than ten years, Hitler was head of state.

The Nazis could not believe how easy it was.
One Nazi wrote: "It all seems like a fairy story."
Hitler said:
"What luck for the rulers that men do not think."

His enemies began to disappear
into concentration camps,
and in a few years he had total power.

The Road to War

When he had killed all his enemies in Germany,
Hitler began to bully other countries.

He said Germany needed to grow
and so he had to take over
Austria, Czechoslovakia and Poland.

He called Britain and France "little worms".
He said they were fools
because they fell for his lies.

Hitler made up his mind
there would be war.
Millions would die,
but he was not afraid of this.

He said it was his duty.

Hitler the Man

Hitler always had tantrums.
As a child, he had fits if he lost an argument.

When he came to power, he got worse.

He thought he was a genius
who was never wrong about anything.
No-one stood up to him,
because they were too frightened.

Hitler thought he was
"one of the most musical people in the world".
When someone told him
he had got a tune wrong,
he said: "No,
it was the composer who went wrong there . . ."

One Nazi told Hitler
he was "more popular than Jesus",
because Jesus had only 12 followers,
and Hitler was loved by all of Germany.

Hitler believed him.

Eva Braun

Eva Braun worked for Hitler's photographer.
She was young and pretty
when Hitler met her.

Hitler liked Eva.
He liked women
who were not as clever as him.
He began to send her flowers.

She told her friends they were in love,
and she would make him marry her.

One day in 1932, when she was 21,
Eva tried to kill herself.

It gave Hitler a shock.
Eva got her way,
and moved in with him.

They were not lovers,
and they never went out together in public.
Sometimes she didn't see him for weeks.
Hitler just kept her,
like something in a collection.

But in time, Hitler became fond of Eva Braun.
When he was with her, he could relax.
She was loyal,
and he called her his "true friend".

In the end, Eva did get Hitler to marry her.
It was at the end of the war, in 1945,
the day before they died together.

By then it didn't matter any more.

War

World War Two
began in September 1939.
It all went well for Germany at first.

Poland fell in 19 days.
Holland, Belgium, Luxemburg and France
all fell in six weeks.

For a time,
Britain was the only country in Europe
still holding out against Hitler's forces.

Just like before,
the success went to Hitler's head.
He attacked Russia in 1941.
(In 1939 he had promised not to attack Russia . . .)

The Germans got to 25 miles from Moscow,
but the Russians held on.
By 1943,
they began to push the Germans back.

By then, America had joined the Allies.
The Germans were out-numbered.
They were being attacked from both sides,
east and west.

Then the Allies landed in France
on D Day, in June 1944.
From then on,
Germany was bound to lose the war.

As usual,
Hitler blamed everyone but himself.

He sent more and more Germans to battle,
to fight and die.
By the end of the war,
there were 14 year-old boys fighting in Berlin.

In the face of defeat,
Hitler stepped up the killing of Jews
in the death camps.

He locked himself away
in his underground bunker,
planning new attacks
with armies which did not exist any more.

He was in a world of his own.
It was only when the Russians were in Berlin,
and the shells were falling on his bunker,
that Hitler began to give in.

The End

In the early hours of 29th April 1945,
the day before he died,
Hitler married Eva Braun.

Next day,
Hitler and his new wife
went into his room.
A few followers waited outside the door.

One shot.

After a while, they went in.
Hitler had shot himself in the head.
He lay covered in blood.

Eva Braun had taken poison.

They took the bodies outside
and set fire to them with petrol.

Next day, the radio said:
"Our Fuhrer Adolf Hitler died for Germany."

Hitler once called himself
"Europe's greatest actor",
because he fooled so many people
into giving him power.

He once boasted that his empire,
the Third Reich,
would last for a thousand years.

In fact, it lasted for 12.

But in those 12 short years,
all over the world,
50 million people had died
in the war that Hitler had started.

Europe's greatest actor
had become
the world's greatest mass murderer.